The World Trade Center

GREAT STRUCTURES IN HISTORY

Other titles in this series

The World Trade Center

GREAT STRUCTURES IN HISTORY

Debbie Levy

KIDHAVEN PRESS

An imprint of Thomson Gale, a part of The Thomson Corporation

THOMSON

™

GALE

Detroit • New York • San Francisco • San Diego • New Haven, Conn.
Waterville, Maine • London • Munich

For more information, contact
KidHaven Press
27500 Drake Rd.
Farmington Hills, MI 48331-3535
Or you can visit our Internet site at http://www.gale.com

LIBRARY OF CONGRESS CATALOGING-IN-PUBLICATION DATA

Levy, Debbie.
  The World Trade Center / by Debbie Levy.
    p. cm. — (Great structures in history)
  Includes bibliographical references and index.
  ISBN 0-7377-2071-9 (hard cover : alk. paper)
  1. World Trade Center (New York, N.Y.)--Juvenile literature. 2. Skyscrapers—New York (State)—New York--Juvenile literature. 3. New York (N.Y.)—Buildings, structures, etc.—Juvenile literature. I. Title. II. Series.
  NA6233.N5W6748 2005
  720'.483'097471—dc22
                                                    2005003011

CONTENTS

CHAPTER ONE

A Very Big Idea

It was spring in New York City, 1966. All the usual signs of the season were in the air. People dug in their small city gardens. Spring breezes blew through the streets.

In one New York City neighborhood, however, the signs of spring were not at all usual. On March 21, the Ajax Wrecking and Lumber Company came to the neighborhood. Its workers approached a one-hundred-year-old brick building and began to tear it down. When they were done with that building, they smashed down another, and another. Eventually, 164 buildings were turned into rubble.

In the rest of crowded New York, the patches of earth that were not covered by buildings were sprouting buds and flowers. But in the neighborhood known as Lower Manhattan, or downtown, something much bigger was about to rise out of the ground.

The work of the wrecking crews marked the beginning of a giant building project. Over the next six years, ten thousand workers labored on the project. They poured

The Twin Towers of the World Trade Center dominated the landscape of Lower Manhattan until they were destroyed by terrorists on September 11, 2001.

425,000 cubic yards (324,936 cubic meters) of concrete. They raised 200,000 tons of steel. The concrete used in the project was enough to build a sidewalk from New York City to Washington, D.C. The amount of steel was more than the amount used to build the 3-mile-long (4.8 kilometer) Verrazano Narrows Bridge across New York Bay.

Power Players

The project that required so many people and so much steel and concrete was the World Trade Center. The World Trade Center was a cluster of seven buildings, but it was much more than that. For a group of powerful businessmen and public officials, it was New York City's future.

The leader of this group was David Rockefeller. He formed the Downtown-Lower Manhattan Association to bring together business leaders interested in transforming downtown New York. Rockefeller was chairman of one of the largest banks in the world, Chase Manhattan Bank. He was a grandson of the nation's first billionaire, John D. Rockefeller. His brother, Nelson Rockefeller, was governor of the state of New York.

David Rockefeller believed that Lower Manhattan needed a makeover. His bank had already built a new headquarters there in 1956, and it would benefit from improvements in the neighborhood. But Rockefeller was not only concerned about improving his bank's surroundings. He also genuinely cared about downtown New York. He began thinking about the World Trade Center in the late 1950s. He wanted to make Lower Manhattan into a place where U.S. and foreign businesses set up offices from

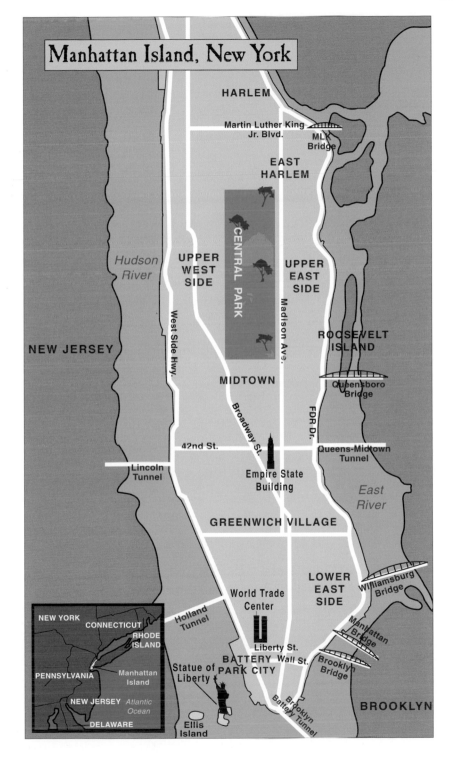

Manhattan Island, New York

HARLEM

Martin Luther King
Jr. Blvd.

MLK
Bridge

EAST
HARLEM

CENTRAL PARK

Hudson
River

UPPER
WEST
SIDE

UPPER
EAST
SIDE

ROOSEVELT
ISLAND

NEW JERSEY

West Side Hwy.

Madison Ave.

Queensboro
Bridge

MIDTOWN

Broadway St.

FDR Dr.

42nd St.

Queens-Midtown
Tunnel

Lincoln
Tunnel

Empire State
Building

East
River

GREENWICH VILLAGE

LOWER
EAST
SIDE

Williamsburg
Bridge

World Trade
Center

Holland
Tunnel

Manhattan
Bridge

Liberty St.

Wall St.

Brooklyn
Bridge

Statue of
Liberty

BATTERY
PARK CITY

Brooklyn
Battery Tunnel

BROOKLYN

NEW YORK

CONNECTICUT

RHODE
ISLAND

PENNSYLVANIA

Manhattan
Island

NEW JERSEY

Atlantic
Ocean

DELAWARE

Ellis
Island

which to conduct global trade. And he had the influence to make his wish come true.

Goodbye, Radio Row

New York City was already a global center of trade and commerce by the time David Rockefeller's association announced plans for the World Trade Center in January 1960. At that time, 7,800,000 people lived in the crowded metropolis. New York City also already had its share of impressive structures. The city's harbor boasted the world-famous Statue of Liberty. Its midtown area (north of down-town) was home to many famous skyscrapers. These included the Empire State Building, which had held the record as the world's tallest building since 1931. In mid-town's skyscrapers, people worked for large corporations, banks, and law offices. Midtown also bustled with the activ-ities of its many stores, restaurants, theaters, and art galleries.

But Lower Manhattan was another story, and that was the focus of Rockefeller's attention. Compared to bustling midtown, New York's downtown area seemed run-down and stagnant. The neighborhood was home to family-owned radio and television stores and other small shops. Local shopkeepers ran their businesses out of old build-ings. David Rockefeller and the other people behind the World Trade Center saw their project as a way to breathe new life into the area. In place of worn, old storefronts, they would build fresh office space, hotel rooms, exhibit halls, and fancy shops. And everything would be wrapped up in a magnificent structure that would make a bold statement about New York's place in the world.

Many downtown shopkeepers liked their neighborhood as it was, especially the merchants who ran the radio and television businesses known as Radio Row. They did not care about making bold statements to the world. They had worked hard to build their businesses on Radio Row. They did not want their stores demolished to make way for someone else's big idea. These merchants opposed the idea of the new World Trade Center. They even fought the plan in court challenges, but they lost their cases. The merchants of Lower Manhattan could not save their small shops and narrow streets from the wrecking crews and from the new vision of New York City's future.

A Fresh Face

A government agency, the Port of New York Authority, took charge of the World Trade Center project in 1961. It

Many buildings in Lower Manhattan had to be torn down to make room for the World Trade Center.

had the power to buy land and destroy existing buildings to make room for the project. One of its other early tasks was to hire an **architect**. Several famous architects competed for the job. Some had already made their mark on New York City, designing such landmarks as the Lincoln Center for the Performing Arts, the United Nations Headquarters, and the General Motors Building.

But in the fall of 1962, the Port Authority selected a lesser-known architect from Detroit, Michigan. His name was Minoru Yamasaki, and he was the son of Japanese immigrants. He often included touches of Japanese beauty in his structures, such as reflecting pools and open spaces. Yamasaki had designed airports from St. Louis to Saudi Arabia. He had not designed a New York skyscraper.

Tall, Taller, Tallest

After visiting the sixteen-acre site where the World Trade Center would stand, Yamasaki went back to his office in Detroit and built a model of Lower Manhattan. His model included all the buildings already there, with an empty space for the World Trade Center site. Then he started drawing up some of his ideas, but he was soon back to models again.

Throughout 1963, Yamasaki and his coworkers built more than one hundred models. Finally, he settled on the idea of two tall towers rising above an outdoor **plaza**. The plaza included sculptures and areas where office workers could sit and enjoy a lunch break. The design included several smaller buildings at the foot of the towers.

Yamasaki's proposed towers were eighty stories tall. They were not taller than the Empire State Building. Yamasaki

Architect Minoru Yamasaki was hired to design the World Trade Center in 1962.

showed his design to Guy Tozzoli, the Port Authority official in charge of the World Trade Center. Tozzoli liked it very much, but he had one request. "I want you to build me the tallest buildings in the world,"[1] Tozzoli said to Yamasaki.

Yamasaki met the challenge. His final design, which was made public in January 1964, included two office towers of 110 stories each. The north tower, with the address One World Trade Center, would be 1,368 feet (417 meters) tall. The south tower, or Two World Trade Center, would rise 1,362 feet (415 meters). The Twin Towers, as they became known, would soar high above everything in Lower Manhattan. They would rise 100 feet (31 meters) taller than the Empire State Building. And they would be taller than any other building in the world.

CHAPTER TWO

Story by Story

Not only did Yamasaki and his team of architects and **engineers** plan to build the world's tallest skyscrapers, they also planned to build their skyscrapers in a totally new way. In the past, skyscrapers had been built using a framework known as a metal skeleton. The skeleton is like a cage of many steel **columns** and **beams**. In this type of skyscraper, so many columns hold up the building on the inside that the outer walls do not need to carry any weight. Because of this, most modern skyscrapers built before the World Trade Center have outer walls made only of glass.

Space and Strength

The designers of the World Trade Center had a different idea. Instead of a steel cage, each skyscraper would have a cluster of columns at its core. Its outer walls would also be made of many columns, spaced just over 1 yard (0.9 meter) apart.

This new design had two advantages. First, the columns scattered throughout a steel-cage skyscraper reduced the amount of floor space available for offices. In the Twin Towers, the floors would be much more open because columns would be clustered at the center and edge of the building, instead of spread throughout.

The second advantage was that the steel columns used to form the outer walls would make the Twin Towers very stable. The skyscrapers would be able to survive winds of 150 miles per hour (241.4 kilometers per hour). Engineers calculated that even if an airplane accidentally crashed into the towers, they would not topple, thanks to the strength of the outer walls.

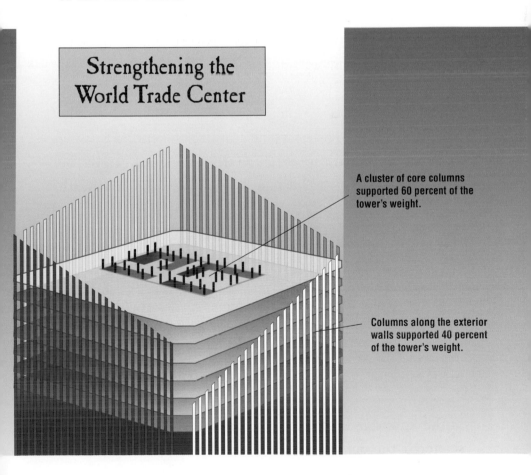

Strengthening the World Trade Center

A cluster of core columns supported 60 percent of the tower's weight.

Columns along the exterior walls supported 40 percent of the tower's weight.

A New Look

Because the new design required so many columns all around the outside of the buildings, the Twin Towers would not look like the glass skyscrapers in New York and other cities. Their windows would be only 22 inches (56 centimeters) wide to fit between the outer columns. The narrow windows and closely spaced columns resembled the ribbing in a pair of corduroy pants.

Many people criticized Yamasaki's design. They said the solid outer walls would be ugly. But supporters of the World Trade Center were pleased. The World Trade Center would look like no other building on Earth, and that was just fine with the people who were bringing it into existence.

Digging Deep

Before the Twin Towers could go up, workers had to dig down, deep into the earth. Tall skyscrapers must be anchored securely into **bedrock**, the solid rock underneath the earth's soil surface. In Lower Manhattan, bedrock lay 70 feet (21.3 meters) below the surface. This created a problem, because Lower Manhattan is also the tip of an island. The Hudson River is on the west side and the East River is on the east side. River water oozes just three feet underground. A hole needed to be dug to a depth of 70 feet, but it would fill with water as quickly as workers could dig it.

Engineers had to figure out a way to keep the water out of the building site. Their solution was to build an underground structure that became known as the "bathtub."

A model of the World Trade Center from 1966 shows the unique look of the Twin Towers, including their narrow windows and closely spaced columns.

Construction of the bathtub began in December 1966. Workers used excavating equipment to dig a trench all around the edge of the building site. The trench was 3 feet (0.9 meter) wide and seven stories deep (about 70 feet, or 21.3 meters). Crews worked on small segments of the trench at a time. Each segment was 22 feet (6.7 meters) long.

As excavators dug dirt and rock out of a segment of trench, other workers quickly poured a mixture of clay (called bentonite) and water into the segment. This mixture, called **slurry**, is very good at absorbing water and plugging holes. The thick slurry stuck to the sides of the trench, absorbing groundwater that would otherwise have seeped in. It kept the trench from filling with groundwater and falling in on itself.

Meanwhile, the excavating equipment continued digging through the slurry down to bedrock. Slurry was poured in constantly as the trench got deeper. Once workers reached bedrock, they were ready to transform the slurry-filled segment of trench into a concrete wall segment. They filled the trench with concrete. As the con-

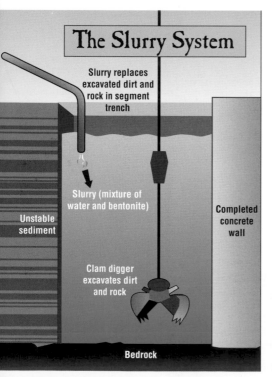

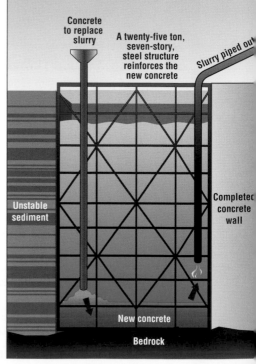

crete flowed in, the slurry was piped out. The concrete hardened, and the result was a solid wall. As additional segments of this wall were completed, a seven-story underground concrete barrier took shape all around the **perimeter** of the building site. This barrier served as a sort of inside-out bathtub that kept water out instead of in. It kept the groundwater of Lower Manhattan out of the space where the World Trade Center would rise.

After fourteen months of nonstop work, the bathtub was completed. In the spring of 1968, the job of **excavating** inside the bathtub began. Excavating machines began scraping out a hole 70 feet (21.3 meters) deep, four city blocks long, and two blocks wide. The 1.2 million cubic yards (917,466 cubic meters) of dirt and rock from the excavation was then moved a few blocks southwest. There, workers used the material to fill in a portion of the Hudson River and create 23 acres (9.3 hectares) of new land. A new neighborhood, called Battery Park City, was created out of dirt from the World Trade Center excavation.

By the summer of 1968, the excavators had finished their job. A gaping hole yawned where streets and buildings used to be. The hole was wide enough to hold sixteen football fields.

The point of digging all the way down to bedrock was to anchor the Twin Towers securely into the earth. A building is anchored, or attached, to the ground by its foundations. To build the foundations for the Twin Towers, workers poured large pads of concrete on the bedrock. Then they installed steel plates and stacks of crisscrossing steel beams on top of each concrete pad. Each

The neighborhood of Battery Park City (pictured) was built on top of dirt excavated from the World Trade Center site.

of the Twin Towers required twenty-eight of these concrete and steel bases.

Going Up

Once the foundations were in place, workers could begin to build upward. Starting with the north tower, they worked from the core of the building to the outside. At the skyscraper's core, workers installed heavy steel columns. Each was seated on one of the twenty-eight concrete-and-steel foundations that had been constructed earlier. The columns were constructed in pieces, so that the core of the building rose a few stories at a time.

Next, workers raised the outer, or exterior, columns. These were constructed from premade sections that were two or three stories high. Laborers then attached floors to these two or three stories, using premade metal sections, concrete, and tile.

Finally, metalworkers attached the outer skin of the skyscrapers to the exterior columns. This skin consisted of large panels of aluminum trimmed with stainless steel. The panels left room for 43,600 windows (21,800 windows per tower), each 22 inches (56 centimeters) wide and tinted a bronze color.

During peak periods of construction activity—1970 and 1971—as many as 3,600 people were on the building site at any given moment. Besides the steelworkers who were raising columns and outside walls, there were electrical

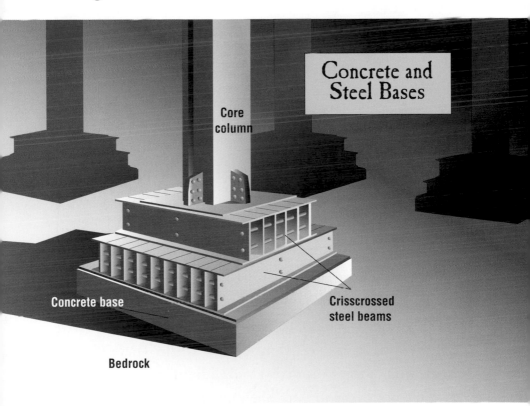

Core column

Concrete and Steel Bases

Concrete base

Crisscrossed steel beams

Bedrock

The north tower of the World Trade Center became the tallest building in the world when it was completed in 1970.

workers, heating and air-conditioning contractors, carpenters, painters, carpet layers, plumbers, window-blind installers, and more. On October 19, 1970, a piece of steel was lifted up to the 103rd floor of the north tower. With that piece of steel, the height of the World Trade Center passed that of the Empire State Building. It was the tallest building in the world—for the moment.

CHAPTER THREE

Life of the Twin Towers

Two months after One World Trade Center (the north tower) set the new world record for height, two small international trading companies became the first occupants of the world's tallest building. As the companies moved in on the tenth and eleventh floors in December 1970, the activity of thousands of construction workers continued all around them. By the following summer, in 1971, both Twin Towers reached their full heights. For two more years, finishing work continued, mostly on the buildings' interiors.

Finally, seven years after ground was broken on the project, the World Trade Center was completed. Public officials and other important people held a ceremony to dedicate the building on April 4, 1973. One month later, the new Sears Tower in Chicago, Illinois, surpassed the Twin Towers in height. Four weeks after its official opening, the World Trade Center no longer contained the tallest buildings in the world.

Still, the Twin Towers were extremely tall skyscrapers by any measure, and the tallest buildings in New York.

Construction on both towers of the World Trade Center was completed in 1973.

They stood as if on guard over Lower Manhattan. Four much smaller buildings—a hotel, a government agency, and two office buildings—completed the complex. (Another smaller building was added in 1987, bringing the number of World Trade Center buildings to seven.)

Many people did not like the finished product. Architecture critics especially did not receive the World Trade Center favorably. Mostly, critics disapproved of the Twin Towers' size (too big) and shape (too boxy and Lego-like). One well-known architecture critic wrote, "These are big buildings, but they are not great buildings."[2]

Coming to Life

Great or a great big mistake, the World Trade Center came to life. By the time it was officially dedicated in early 1973, its offices were half-filled. Like a miniature city, the World Trade Center had its own subway stop, commuter train station, stores, barbershops, restaurants, and police force. It had nine chapels where people of different religions could worship. It even had its own postal service ZIP code: 10048.

Soon, the World Trade Center began to hum with the activities of all sorts of businesses. Insurance companies, banks, and stockbrokers moved in. Engineering firms, accounting firms, and law firms got to work. Publishers, airlines, and charitable organizations settled in. Foreign businesses and governments set up offices in the World Trade Center. Before long, more than four hundred businesses or organizations had offices there. They ranged from the Royal Thai Embassy (of Thailand) to Fuji Bank

Every day thousands of people came to work at the World Trade Center, where hundreds of businesses had offices.

(of Japan) to Kemper Insurance Companies (of the United States). Every morning, around fifty thousand people came to work in the Twin Towers and the other buildings in the World Trade Center.

Center of Attention

New Yorkers may not have loved the Twin Towers on sight, but they were drawn to them anyway. They came to ride the high-speed elevator in the south tower, which took them to an observation deck on the 107th floor. From there, they could gaze through the windows in every direction, for 40 miles (64 kilometers) on a clear day. Adventuresome visitors could take an additional escalator ride to an outdoor deck on top of the south tower's roof. The Port Authority advertised the observation deck, which opened in 1975, with the slogan "It's hard to be down when you are up."[3]

New Yorkers and other visitors to the city also were attracted to Windows on the World, a fancy restaurant that opened in 1976 on the 107th floor of the north tower. Restaurant critics praised the restaurant, both for its food and for its spectacular views. For visitors more interested in fashion than food, the shopping mall in the basement of the World Trade Center offered its own attractions. Every day, more than one hundred thousand visitors came to the World Trade Center to shop, sightsee, eat, or do business.

Tourists take in the spectacular view from the World Trade Center's observation deck on the 107th floor.

Daredevils' Delight

The Twin Towers also proved irresistible to daredevils. For them, the World Trade Center was a perfect place to perform thrilling, and unauthorized, stunts. The first of these daredevils was Philippe Petit, a twenty-four-year-old juggler and magician from France. He spent months planning to walk between the north and south tower, a distance of 131 feet (39.9 meters), on a tightrope. On August 7, 1974, he carried out his feat. Petit and some friends had previously disguised themselves as construction workers to gain entry to the building and to bring cables, a crossbow, and other equipment to the top floors. They used the crossbow to shoot a line between the north and south towers, and then strung a heavy cable along the line.

Despite strong winds, Petit set off on his tightrope walk at 7:15 A.M. He carried a 38-foot (11.5 meters) long balancing pole. For more than an hour he walked back and forth across the cable, occasionally stopping to lie on, sit on, or hang from the high wire. A crowd of people on the street stopped to watch the amazing and dangerous stunt, creating a large traffic jam. Later, Petit explained, "When I see two towers, I just want to put my wire across, *bon* [good]!"[4] New York City officials were so happy with the favorable attention Petit drew to the Twin Towers that they did not even punish him.

Other thrill seekers followed. A skydiver named Owen Quinn got past building guards to parachute from the top of the north tower to the ground below in July 1975. And in 1977, a toy designer and mountain climber named George Willig climbed up the exterior of the south tower.

In 1974 French daredevil Philippe Petit walked on a tightrope between the Twin Towers.

Like Petit, Willig also planned his stunt for months. He made special climbing clamps to fit inside the tracks that ran up and down the outside of the tower to hold window-washing equipment.

Using his clamps, a harness, and a bright blue nylon rope, Willig started his climb around 6:30 A.M. on May 27, 1977. A large crowd gathered in the streets and plaza to watch. When one spectator wondered aloud, "What's holding him up?" a police officer replied, "A lot of guts."[5] About three and a half hours later, Willig reached the top of the skyscraper, where he was met by police officers. Although Willig was arrested, the mayor of New York decided that the stunt did not deserve punishment. Willig was only required to pay a fine of $1.10—one penny for every floor he climbed. He became known as the Human Fly.

Slowly but surely, the World Trade Center gained the acceptance, and even the affection, of many New Yorkers and visitors to the city. The Twin Towers were pictured on countless postcards and posters. They were featured in movies and television shows. Souvenirs such as key chains, pencil sharpeners, and thermometers were plastered with images of the World Trade Center. All around the globe, people knew what it was.

Terror from the Skies

The World Trade Center was never just a group of office buildings. To many, the World Trade Center became a symbol not only of New York, but also of America. It stood for American **economic power** and American **culture**.

The problem with being a center of attention is that sometimes the attention paid is undesirable. The World Trade Center attracted the attention of people who viewed the United States as an enemy and who wished to harm it.

Basement Bombing

Shortly after noon on February 26, 1993, a powerful bomb exploded in the parking garage underneath the Twin Towers. Six people died in the explosion. One thousand others were injured. The people who planned the bombing wanted to strike at the American system of government and its economy. The **terrorists** chose the World Trade Center because it was such a famous symbol. They had hoped to topple the Twin Towers, but the blast did not

For many people, the World Trade Center was a powerful symbol of American culture.

damage the upper floors at all. The buildings were repaired in two months. Six terrorists were convicted of crimes and sent to prison for their roles in the bombing.

Some things changed at the World Trade Center after the 1993 bombing. An emergency command center was set up in each building. Guards checked entry to the World Trade Center more carefully than before.

None of these safeguards changed life very much for people who worked at the World Trade Center. More importantly, none of them stopped the attack on the Twin Towers that came out of the sky on September 11, 2001.

Twin Crashes

At 8:46 A.M. on September 11, American Airlines Flight 11 crashed into the north tower of the World Trade Center. The plane burst into the building between the ninety-fourth and ninety-ninth floors. Smoke and fire immediately engulfed that portion of the skyscraper. At 9:02 A.M. a second airplane, United Airlines Flight 175, smashed into the south tower between the seventy-eighth and eighty-fourth floors. The impact of the jet created a huge orange fireball.

Brian Clark worked for a company on the eighty-fourth floor of the south tower. When the second jet struck his building, he told a reporter for the Public Broadcasting Service, "For seven to ten seconds there was this enormous sway in the building. It was one way, and I just felt in my heart, *Oh my gosh, we are going over.* That's what it felt like."[6]

The Twin Towers swayed from the tremendous impact of the jets, but they did not fall over. Many people working

The south tower explodes in a ball of fire as a second hijacked airplane crashes into the World Trade Center on September 11, 2001.

in the skyscrapers below the floors where the airplanes hit rushed to the stairwells and began a long trek down to the ground floor. Others stayed in their offices, perhaps reassured by the fact that the buildings had survived the crashes. The people on the floors above the impact of the planes were nearly all trapped. They could not walk downstairs through the blazing, smoking sites of the explosions. All they could do was wait.

The Unimaginable

Firefighters, ambulance drivers, paramedics, and police rushed to the scene. Many entered the Twin Towers to fight the flames and help people escape. Telephone lines in New York and other areas were clogged as people tried to call loved ones and friends. Television stations quickly sent crews to film the tragedy.

Then the unimaginable happened. As millions watched on television, the south tower collapsed at 9:59 A.M. Starting slowly at first, the skyscraper caved in on itself. As the upper stories fell on those beneath it, the broken columns, beams, and floors gained force and speed. By the time the upper floors hit the ground, they were traveling downward at 120 miles per hour (193.1 kilometers per

Hundreds of firefighters rushed to Ground Zero to battle fires and help victims escape from the collapsing towers.

hour). Half an hour later, the north tower met the same fate. The skyscrapers that had once soared high above the city had practically disappeared. Their tons of steel, miles of wires, and acres of floors had been squeezed into piles of rubble.

Around twenty-five thousand people escaped from the burning towers. Approximately three thousand people were killed. Many died in the initial crash. Others were killed by flames and smoke as fuel from the jets continued to burn. Still more, including rescue workers, were crushed and buried when the Twin Towers collapsed. In addition to the Twin Towers, three other buildings that made up the World Trade Center were destroyed.

The destruction of the Twin Towers was no accident. Both jets involved in the tragedy were supposed to be traveling from Boston, Massachusetts, to Los Angeles, California. Both had been **hijacked**, or taken over, by terrorists disguised as passengers. The terrorists used the airplanes as weapons and intentionally steered them into the Twin Towers. At around the same time, other terrorists hijacked two other airplanes. One crashed into the Pentagon building outside the Washington, D.C. The other crashed into a field in Pennsylvania. All nineteen of the hijackers died in the crashes, along with all the innocent passengers on the targeted flights. September 11, 2001, marked the deadliest attack on the United States in its history.

Fury of Fire

When the Twin Towers were designed in the 1960s, its engineers said they could survive the force of being hit by an airplane. The collapse, however, does not necessarily prove that the engineers designed unsafe structures. Experts point out that the Twin Towers were designed not to fall over if struck by a typical commercial airplane of the late 1960s—and they did not fall over on September 11. However, the engineers who designed the Twin Towers did not have in mind such large airplanes, fully loaded with enough fuel to fly from Massachusetts to California. The thousands of gallons of jet fuel set off huge fires. These intense fires caused the steel in the columns and floors to weaken. And once the weakened upper floors started falling on the floors below, the buildings were crushed from the top. Each floor collapsed on the one underneath it.

After the Disaster

Immediately after the collapse, rescue workers began looking for survivors. They picked their way carefully around the smoking remains of the skyscrapers. The area quickly became known as "Ground Zero." By September 12, twenty-one people were found alive. The search continued for two more weeks. No other survivors were found.

For eight more months, workers continued to comb through Ground Zero. They were no longer looking for survivors. Their job was to recover the bodies of the people who died in the collapse of the World Trade Center. They also collected truckloads of rubble—108,000 truckloads in total—which went to Staten Island, New York. There, experts sorted through the rubble, looking for clues to explain the disaster.

Rescue workers at Ground Zero dig through the rubble in search of survivors of the September 11 terrorist attacks.

By June 2002, the recovery work at Ground Zero was over. Everything that could be recovered from the site had been recovered. Items included more than seventy-five thousand dollars in U.S. and foreign money and fifty-four thousand personal objects such as photographs, drivers' licenses, wallets, and cell phones belonging to people who had worked in the World Trade Center. Many of these were given to the families of those who died.

New York City's leaders and citizens next turned to the question of rebuilding Ground Zero. In 2004, work began on the Freedom Tower, a skyscraper 1,776 feet (541 meters) tall. The tower was designed to rise even taller than the Twin Towers. Like the Twin Towers, the Freedom Tower was intended to make a statement. The message was that the terrorist attacks of September 11 did not crush the spirit of New Yorkers or Americans. The design for the project included a memorial to honor those who died there.

In its brief existence, the World Trade Center made a lasting impression. The destruction of the World Trade Center also made a lasting impression. In October 2001, the U.S. government invaded Afghanistan because its leaders had supported the terrorist groups involved in the September 11 attacks. The World Trade Center tragedy also led the U.S. government to launch a general "war on terror." President George W. Bush used the war on terror as a reason to invade Iraq in 2003. As a result of the World Trade Center attacks, the United States changed the way airports are run, created the Department of Homeland Security, and developed a terror alert system.

In 2003 officials unveil a model of the Freedom Tower that is currently under construction on the site of the World Trade Center.

All this was very different from the vision of the future that inspired those who dreamed up the World Trade Center in the 1960s. But if the structure they created has been erased from the tip of Manhattan, it has certainly not been erased from the minds of Americans or others around the globe.

Notes

Chapter 1: A Very Big Idea

1. Quoted in Angus Kress Gillespie, *Twin Towers: The Life of New York City's World Trade Center*. New Brunswick, NJ: Rutgers University Press, 1999, p. 48.

Chapter 3: Life of the Twin Towers

2. Quoted in Bill Harris, *The World Trade Center: A Tribute*. Philadelphia: Courage Books, 2001, p. 57.

3. Quoted in James Glanz and Eric Lipton, *City in the Sky: The Rise and Fall of the World Trade Center*. New York: Times Books, p. 220.

4. Quoted in Glanz and Lipton, *City in the Sky*, p. 219.

5. Quoted in Glanz and Lipton, *City in the Sky*, p. 218.

Chapter 4: Terror from the Skies

6. Quoted in NOVA Online, "Above the Impact: A Survivor's Story." www.pbs.org/wgbh/nova/wtc.

Glossary

architect: A person who designs and oversees the construction of buildings.

beams: Long pieces of steel used as part of the frame or skeleton of a building.

bedrock: The solid rock underneath the earth's soil.

columns: Slender vertical structures, or pillars, that usually support something above them in a building.

culture: The arts, beliefs, and knowledge that are common to a particular community, nation, or group of people.

economic power: Strength that comes from wealth, such as the wealth of a nation.

engineers: People who are trained in engineering, or the use of science and math to create or improve projects and inventions, such as buildings and bridges.

excavating: Digging a hole.

hijacked: Taken by force.

perimeter: The outer boundary of an area or structure.

plaza: A public square or other space, often set aside in a city for people to enjoy the outdoors.

slurry: A mixture of water and clay.

terrorists: People who perform acts of terrorism, or violence that is aimed at governments, often for political reasons.

For Further Reading

Books

Laurel Corona, *The World Trade Center*. San Diego, CA: Lucent, 2002. This informative account of the building of the World Trade Center includes a time line and sidebars with unusual facts and figures about the structure.

Gini Holland, *The Empire State Building*. New York: Raintree-Steck-Vaughn, 1998. Photographs and illustrations bring to life the story of one of the world's most famous skyscrapers.

Carol A. Johmann, *Skyscrapers! Super Structures to Design and Build*. Charlotte, VT: Williamson, 2001. Readers can learn about every step in the planning and creation of a skyscraper in this book. Hands-on activities and experiments are included.

Peter Kent, *Great Building Stories of the Past*. New York: Oxford University Press, 2001. With detailed pictures, this book tells the stories of nine amazing structures around the world, from the Brooklyn Bridge to the Great Wall of China.

Frank Walsh, *New York City*. Milwaukee, WI: World Almanac Library, 2004. New York City's past, present, and future are covered in this book, which includes photographs and maps.

Web Sites

The Great Buildings Collection (www.greatbuildings. com). This Web site offers detailed, beautiful photographs of famous buildings, including the World Trade Center. Links to related Web sites are also offered.

NOVA Online: Why The Towers Fell (www.pbs.org/ wgbh/nova/wtc). The events of September 11, 2001, are explored in detail, with expert analysis of the collapse of the Twin Towers. The Web site includes an in-depth interview with a World Trade Center worker who survived the tragedy.

Public Broadcasting Service: Building Big (www.pbs. org/wgbh/buildingbig/index.html). Skyscrapers, domes, bridges, tunnels, and dams are the subjects of this site. The challenges of building skyscrapers are examined with the help of interactive problems. The site also includes a "Wonders of the World Databank," with information about famous structures around the world.

Index

Picture Credits

Cover: © Ron Watts/CORBIS

© AFP/Getty Images, 40
AP Wide World Photos, 7, 22, 24, 29
© Bettmann/CORBIS, 13
© David Ball/CORBIS, 20
© Gail Mooney/CORBIS, 27
© Hulton Archive/Getty Images, 11, 17
© James Marshall/Lonely Planet Images, 32
   Naomi Stock/Landov, 34
© Neville Elder/CORBIS, 35
Maury Aaseng, 9
U.S. Navy photo by Photographer's Mate 2nd Class
   Jim Watson, 38
© Viviane Moos/CORBIS, 26

About the Author

Before she started writing books for children, Debbie Levy earned a bachelor's degree in government and foreign affairs from the University of Virginia, as well as a law degree and master's degree in world politics from the University of Michigan. She practiced law with a large Washington, D.C., law firm and worked as a newspaper editor. Her previous books for children include books for KidHaven Press, Lucent Books, and Blackbirch Press, on such topics as the Berlin Wall, sunken treasure, slave life, Maryland, civil liberties, bigotry, and medical ethics. Debbie enjoys paddling around in kayaks and canoes and fishing in the Chesapeake Bay region. She lives with her husband, two sons, dog, and cat in Maryland.